AMERICA IN WORLD WAR II

EDWARD F. DOLAN

THE MILLBROOK PRESS
BROOKFIELD, CONNECTICUT

Cover photograph courtesy of the National Archives

Photos courtesy of UPI/Bettmann: pp. 4, 56 (both),
60, 66 (both); the National Archives: pp. 11, 13
(top), 16, 25 (both), 26, 27, 42, 45, 53, 55, 58,
64 (both); Keystone Press: p. 13 (bottom); Sov-
foto: p. 18; Wide World Photos: pp. 28, 37, 39;
Carl Mydans, Life Magazine © Time, Inc.: p. 33;
U.S. Marine Corps: p. 36; Los Alamos National
Laboratory: p. 48. Maps by Joe LeMonnier.

Library of Congress Cataloging-in-Publication Data
(Revised for vol. 5)
Dolan, Edward F., 1924–
America in World War II.
Includes bibliographical references and index.
Contents: — [3] 1943— [etc.]—[5] 1945
1. World War, 1939–1945—Campaigns—Juvenile
literature.   2. World War, 1939–1945—United
States—Juvenile literature.   3. World War, 1939–
1945—United States. I. America in World War 2.
II. America in World War Two.   III. Title.
D743.7.D65 1992 940.54′1   91-30808
ISBN 1-56294-320-0 (v. [5])

Published by The Millbrook Press
2 Old New Milford Road, Brookfield, Conn. 06804

CONTENTS

INTRODUCTION: THE STORY THUS FAR

America was thrust into World War II on December 7, 1941. Without warning, Japanese planes that day bombed six U.S. military installations on the Hawaiian island of Oahu. Chief among the targets was the giant Pearl Harbor naval base. Hours later, U.S. bases in the Philippine Islands and on the islands of Wake, Guam, and Midway were bombed. Also hit were British outposts along the Pacific edge of Asia.

The attacks marked the latest steps in Japan's campaign to become the most powerful nation in Asia. It was a campaign that had begun in 1931, when Japan had invaded China. China had been fighting the invaders ever since.

On December 8, 1941, an outraged United States declared war on Japan. Japan's allies—Germany and Italy—then declared war on America. The United States answered with a return declaration. Great Britain, which was already at war in Europe with Germany and Italy, joined America in the fight against Japan. The European conflict had erupted in 1939 when German dictator Adolf Hitler invaded Poland.

THE WAR IN THE PACIFIC ▪ In the closing weeks of 1941, Japanese troops captured the islands of Wake and Guam, and invaded the Philippines. The first months of 1942 saw the

Nazi leader Adolf Hitler surveys bomb damage in a German town. By the start of 1945, when this undated photograph was released, Allied troops were massed on Germany's western border.

invaders crush the defenders of the Philippines and win control of the islands. But June brought a major U.S. victory at the island of Midway deep in the North Pacific.

The victory showed that the American forces were regaining their strength after being hurt at Pearl Harbor. In the next months, they undertook two major campaigns against the enemy. Heading the first was the Army's General Douglas MacArthur. The second was commanded by the Navy's Admiral Chester W. Nimitz.

MacArthur launched his campaign in late 1942 and spent all of 1943 attacking and capturing a number of enemy-held islands north of Australia. These attacks were meant to clear the enemy from his path so that he could move freely toward his principal target, the Philippine Islands. Once he had won back the Philippines, he could strike north at Japan itself.

Like MacArthur, Nimitz was heading for Japan, and, in the first nine months of 1944, he captured a string of islands that brought him ever closer to his objective. But then he broke off the move toward the enemy homeland. MacArthur was now ready to invade the Philippines, and Nimitz sent his ships sailing close to the islands to provide the general with support.

The Philippine invasion took place in October 1944. MacArthur's troops stormed ashore on the island of Leyte. Next, in December, he sent them against the island of Mindoro. It fell to them just before Christmas.

Mindoro lay at the foot of Luzon, the largest island in the Philippine chain and the home of its capital city, Manila. As 1945 dawned, the general was preparing to invade Luzon. And Admiral Nimitz had his ships again moving north toward Japan.

THE WAR IN EUROPE ▪ America's participation in the European war did not begin in Europe itself but in North Africa. In November 1942, a giant U.S. and British force invaded North Africa and began to drive the Germans out of Morocco, Algeria, and Tunisia. The purpose of the invasion was to give the Allies a base from which to launch attacks against southern Europe. (The terms *Allies* and *Allied* were used in the war to denote the nations fighting Germany, Italy, and Japan.) The North African campaign came to a successful close in May 1943.

Next, the British and U.S. troops crossed the Mediterranean Sea in July and took the island of Sicily just off the southwestern tip of Italy. In September, they moved into Italy itself. The nation immediately withdrew from the war, but the German forces there continued to fight on. Throughout the rest of 1943 and all of 1944, the Allies battled their way north through Italy.

Mid-1944 brought an invasion far to the west of Italy. On June 6, more than 5,300 ships—troop transports, supply vessels, and warships—sailed across the English Channel from Great Britain to the beaches at Normandy, France. U.S., British, and Canadian soldiers waded ashore and moved inland to beat back the German defenders. In charge of the operation was America's General Dwight D. Eisenhower, the commander of all Allied troops in Europe.

In August, the invaders were joined by U.S. and French troops that sailed in from the Mediterranean and landed on the southern coast of France. For the rest of the year, the Allies spread through France—east to the German border and north into the enemy-held countries of Belgium, Luxembourg, and Holland. By December, their front line extended more than 200 miles down the German frontier from Holland and Belgium to the Saar region. The Saar was a vital German industrial area.

Eisenhower wanted to continue eastward immediately and cross one of Germany's major rivers, the Rhine. Before a full-scale advance on the river could be made, winter closed in with heavy snows. It was then that the Germans, after months of retreating before the Allies, struck back. In mid-December, Hitler sent a massive force out of Germany and threw it against the U.S. troops stationed along the Belgium and Luxembourg borders. His plan was to have his men plunge all the way across Belgium to the port city of Antwerp, which the Allies had captured earlier in the year. If successful, the attack would drive a wedge between the British and American troops in northern Europe and would retake the city that was now serving as the chief port for the landing of their supplies. This, Hitler thought, would soon bring the war to an end in his favor.

The next weeks proved him wrong. At first, catching the Americans by surprise, his troops drove a deep wedge into Belgium. This caused the Americans to call the attack ''The Battle of the Bulge.'' But, late in the month, the Americans stopped the assault at several points, a chief one being the city of Bastogne. From then on, they steadily pushed the enemy troops back.

The German attack had ended in dismal failure. The final months of the war in Europe were at hand. . . .

ONE:
THE ATTACK ON
THE RHINE

With the Battle of the Bulge won, General Eisenhower returned to his plan to reach the Rhine River. In February 1945 he sent his troops moving all along the front they had established in the days before the Bulge. The front ran from Holland in the north to the Saar region in the south.

TO THE RHINE ▪ For the attack, Eisenhower divided his forces into three main units, called Groups. They were the 21st, 12th, and 6th Army Groups. Their first job was to reach the Rhine's west bank. Once it was in their hands, they would thrust across the river. Eisenhower assigned the northern section of the front to the 21st Army Group. It was made up of three armies—the Canadian 1st, the British 2nd, and the American 9th—all under the command of Britain's Field Marshal Bernard Law Montgomery.

Jumping off from the area around the Dutch city of Nijmegen, Montgomery's men began their attack on February 8. At first, they advanced with agonizing slowness because they had to struggle across canals and small rivers swollen with the waters from an early thaw. All the while, they faced a stubborn, hard-fighting enemy. But as the days passed, the German defenders began to fall away before them and they quickened their pace. On February 14, they reached the Rhine near the Germany city of Wesel.

The 12th Army Group, headed by America's Lt. General Omar N. Bradley, struck along the center section of the front. Under him were two U.S. armies—the 1st and the 3rd. They began their attack on February 23 and drove through the Siegfried Line to the cities of Cologne, Coblenz, and Mainz. On March 4, the 1st Army reached the outskirts of Cologne and took the city on March 7 after three days of vicious street-to-street fighting.

To the south, the 3rd Army, commanded by the fiery Lt. General George S. Patton, crashed into Coblenz on March 9 after days of fighting that saw his men take 4,500 prisoners. From there, Patton's tanks and infantry rolled south to Mainz. The city fell to them on March 22.

Responsible for the southern section of the front was the 6th Army Group. Commanded by America's Lt. General Jacob Devers, it was made up of the U.S. 7th Army and the French 1st Army. This Group had the job of driving the enemy out of the industrial Saar region, a task that the 7th Army completed when it captured the cities of Zweibrucken and Saarbrucken. Both cities were in American hands by March 20.

All German resistance along the western bank of the Rhine had now collapsed. Eisenhower was ready to surge across the river and into the heart of Germany.

THE BRIDGE AT REMAGEN ▪ The attack across the Rhine began on March 23. Actually, by that day, men from two U.S. units were already on the far side of the river. On the night of March 22, after taking Mainz, General Patton sent one of

An American soldier stands amid ruins in the city of Cologne, Germany.

his divisions over to the eastern bank. He jokingly reported to General Bradley that the retreating Germans had left so few men behind that he was sure the enemy didn't even know he had arrived.

Another U.S. outfit, however, had crossed the river sixteen days ahead of Patton. Men from the 1st Army had made their way over to the eastern bank on March 7, when they had swept across a bridge at the small town of Remagen.

In late February, on orders from Hitler, the German field commanders had begun dynamiting the bridges all along the Rhine so that the Allies would not be able to dash across them. By the first days of March, the river was scarred with one twisted and collapsed span after another. Vessels of all types—barges, rafts, and small boats—crowded the surrounding waters. Some carried retreating troops to the safety of the eastern bank. Others hauled ammunition and supplies to troops still battling the Allied advance.

Only a few bridges remained intact and were being used as escape routes for tanks and trucks. One of their number was the Ludendorff Bridge at Remagen. Just over 1,000 feet in length, it was named in honor of General Erich von Ludendorff, a leading commander in World War I. On its eastern side, the bridge ended at the base of a 600-foot-high bluff. A tunnel ran through the bluff.

On the morning of March 7, the bridge was guarded by 1,000 exhausted German soldiers. The span was meant for railroad traffic only, and they had spent the past days covering its tracks over with planks so that it could be used by the retreating tanks and trucks. Then, all through the preceding night, they had planted explosive charges—sixty in all—along its length. When their work was done, their commander,

Left: General Dwight D. Eisenhower, the commander of Allied forces in Europe, with Lt. General Omar N. Bradley and Lt. General George S. Patton in February 1945. Below: The Ludendorff Bridge at Remagen, seen from the western bank of the Rhine. German soldiers were positioned on the tall bluff on the opposite bank of the river.

Captain Willi Bratge, stationed them on top of the bluff and in the tunnel. Now, pale and dirty, the men awaited the arrival of the Allied troops. Captain Bratge was under orders not to trigger the explosive charges until the very last moment so that the Ludendorff could serve as an escape route for as long as possible. That "very last moment" was sure to come very soon, he knew. He could hear the thunder of the Allied guns rolling nearer and nearer.

A small contingent of 1st Army soldiers reached a hilltop above Remagen early in the afternoon. Far below was a sight that astonished them: an undamaged bridge stretching across the Rhine and alive with traffic moving eastward. They immediately sent word of their find back to their commander.

When he arrived on the hilltop, he quickly saw the dangers his men would face if they attempted to take the bridge. There were enemy soldiers entrenched on the bluff at its far end—and most likely others hidden in the tunnel. They would loose a deadly fire on anyone who dared approach the span.

But he knew his men would have to risk a crossing. The bridge, offering a quick route across the Rhine for all the troops coming up behind him, was too good a prize to miss. He called for an artillery barrage on the span. Shells began pouring out of the hills. But they did not strike their target and tear it to pieces. Rather, they were timed to burst in the air and send white-hot metal fragments raining down on the tanks, trucks, and uniformed figures fleeing toward the eastern bank.

During the barrage, the men who had first sighted the bridge inched their way down to the river. On arriving, they did not attempt an immediate crossing. Rather, they were under orders to wait until reinforced by comrades who were now surging through Remagen. The reinforcements swept into view a short time later. Then smoke bombs began to rain in from the hills above the town. The men knew that the time for the crossing was at hand. The smoke from the bombs was meant to hide them from the enemy's view as they moved forward.

Over the eastern bank, Captain Bratge watched the Americans mass for the coming attack and saw the first of the smoke bombs explode. The last of the German tanks had made their way across and the Ludendorff was free of traffic. That "very last moment" had arrived. But when one of his officers tried to activate the device that would detonate the sixty charges on the span, there were no explosions. The barrage of air-burst shells had damaged the lines leading to the charges. A sergeant now dashed out onto the bridge and put a match to the fuse leading to a large emergency charge. As he came running back through the smoke, the bridge shuddered with a heavy explosion. But it did not collapse. The charge did nothing but carve a hole in its roadbed.

The 1st Army men now charged onto the span. Captain Bratge attempted to halt the charge by leading a group of soldiers to a ledge above the tunnel entrance so that he could fire down on the attackers. But the American rifle fire drove him off. Moments later, he knew that all was lost. More and more American troops were storming toward him. He could not turn them back. The Ludendorff Bridge was theirs. He ordered his men to surrender.

By dusk, more than 100 Americans were across the Ludendorff. They were joined in the next days by some 8,000 men who spread out to establish a foothold along the east side of the Rhine. By the time the major crossing of the river began on March 23, that foothold would measure 25 miles long by 10 miles deep.

TWO:
THE DEATH OF
HITLER'S GERMANY

Once the Allied troops began to cross the Rhine, Hitler's Germany was doomed. The nation was being squeezed to death between two giant forces—Eisenhower's armies from the west and a host of Soviet armies from the east.

Hitler had invaded Russia in 1941 and had pushed deep into the nation before finally being stopped at the cities of Moscow, Leningrad, and Stalingrad. In 1943, Soviet troops began to drive his forces back out. The drive continued throughout 1944. By March 1945, the Germans were gone from Russia and the Soviets were attacking them along a front that extended all the way down the eastern face of Europe. Beginning in Germany's East Prussia, it ran south through Poland, Czechoslovakia, Hungary, and Yugoslavia. One Soviet army, commanded by Marshal Georgy Zhukov, was over the German border near the German capital, Berlin, and was surging toward the city.

ACROSS THE RHINE ▪ March 23 marked the first major crossing of the Rhine. That day, General Montgomery's 12th Army Group—the U.S. 9th Army, British 2nd, and Canadian 1st—took to boats and made their way over to the city of Wesel. They reached the east bank against light resistance and looked

U.S. Army troops cross the Rhine on March 23, 1945.

up to see waves of aircraft roaring in to drop 14,000 American and British paratroopers and glidermen behind the enemy lines.

Facing such a light enemy resistance, the ground and airborne troops soon linked up and pressed into the Ruhr district. Like the Saar far to the south, the Ruhr was a region of coal mines and steel and iron plants. The loss of the area would join the loss of the Saar in reducing what little strength the dying Germany had left.

Directly to Montgomery's south, the U.S. 1st Army attacked out of its foothold on the east bank of the Rhine at Remagen and joined Patton's 3rd Army in rushing to the city of Frankfurt. Still farther south, the U.S. 7th Army crossed over on March 27, with the French 1st following on April 1. The last of Eisenhower's forces were now beyond the river. He immediately ordered a series of new moves.

First, he had a number of units from the U.S. 9th Army turn south from Wesel and swing down the east side of the Ruhr district. At the same time, he sent elements of the U.S.

MARSHAL GEORGY ZHUKOV

Marshal Zhukov commanded the Soviet troops that captured Berlin. German soldiers and civilians were terrified of all the Soviet units advancing from the east. Many fled to the Allied lines.

THE ALLIED
ADVANCE
FROM THE WEST

→ British and
Canadian Armies

→ American and
French Armies

North
Sea

Kiel

Hamburg

Wismar

Bremen

Berlin

Amsterdam

NETHERLANDS

Hannover

Arnhem

Münster

Brunswick

GERMANY

British 21st Group

Wesel

Paderborn

Göttingen

Brussels

Dortmund

Essen

Kassel

Dessau

Liepzig

Aachen

Cologne

Liege

Bonn

U.S. 12th Group

Remagen

BELGIUM

Koblenz

Frankfurt

Mainz

U.S. 6th Group

Mannheim

FRANCE

Nancy

Nuremberg

Stuttgart

Munich

Zurich

SWITZERLAND

AUSTRIA

ITALY

0   100 Miles

0   150 Kilometers

1st Army curving along the southern edge of the Ruhr from their foothold at Remagen. The action saw the two groups meet on April 3 and form a circle around the Ruhr and its major cities, among them Dortmund and Essen. Two weeks of vicious fighting followed as the Americans slowly pressed in on the center of the circle. When the fighting ended, some 325,000 enemy soldiers were prisoners of the Americans.

Eisenhower made his next moves while the Ruhr was being encircled. First, he instructed Montgomery to march his British and Canadian forces out from Wesel. Some were to advance into northern Germany, with its cities of Bremen and Hamburg. Others were to seek out the enemy troops still in Holland and Denmark.

Next, the U.S. 9th and 1st Armies, leaving behind the units that were encircling the Ruhr, were sent racing eastward across Germany. Moving alongside them was Patton's 3rd Army. Their dash was aimed at the Elbe River near the Polish and Czechoslovakian borders. The general's plan here was to split Germany apart along an east-west line. This would keep the enemy troops in the southern part of the nation from rushing up to assist their comrades in the north, especially those in Berlin. The city was now coming under attack from the east by the Soviet troops under the command of Marshal Georgy Zhukov.

Finally, Eisenhower sent orders to the U.S. 7th Army and the French 1st Army at the southern end of his front. He told them to work their way down to the Bavarian Alps. The general ordered the move after receiving intelligence reports that the Germans were planning to mass 100,000 men there for a final stand. He hoped that the American and French troops could put an end to the plan before it had a chance to materialize.

THE YALTA CONFERENCE ▪ As the 1st, 3rd, and 9th Armies sped across Germany to the Elbe, many of their number thought they were heading for Berlin. But they soon learned they were not to go near the city. This was because of a decision that had been recently made by the Allied leaders —U.S. President Franklin Roosevelt, British Prime Minister Winston Churchill, and Soviet Premier Joseph Stalin.

The trio had met several times over the course of the European war to discuss its progress. Their latest meeting had taken place early this year, in February, at the Russian city of Yalta. There, they had agreed on a number of military and political plans for the future. One of the plans called for Germany to be divided into four zones at war's end. Each of the Allied powers—America, Great Britain, the Soviet Union, and France—was to be given a zone to govern. Berlin stood within the zone assigned to the Soviets, so its capture was to be left to Marshal Zhukov, with Eisenhower staying well to its south.

The three leaders reached a series of other agreements at the Yalta Conference:

- The Allies would accept nothing less than an unconditional surrender from Hitler.

- Germany was to pay reparations for the damages done in the fighting; the nation's war industries were to be eliminated; and the most brutal of the country's leaders were to be tried as criminals.

- Stalin was to declare war on Japan (he had never done so) when the European fighting ended. In return, he was to be given a number of Japanese-held islands off the east coast of Russia. In other agreements, certain areas in eastern Europe were placed under his control.

Roosevelt, Churchill, and Stalin ended the Yalta Conference with a joint statement concerning the founding of an international organization. It was to work for world peace in the coming years by seeking an enduring cooperation among nations everywhere. The organization had been discussed by various nations since 1942, and the three leaders now announced that definite steps should be taken to bring it into being. Their announcement led to an international meeting that opened on April 25, 1945, at San Francisco, California. It ended two months later when representatives of fifty countries signed the charter that gave birth to the United Nations.

APRIL VICTORIES AND HORRORS ▪ Eisenhower's moves into Germany netted him one victory after another in April. Montgomery's troops swept into northern Germany, capturing the city of Bremen by month's end and then Hamburg in early May. The U.S. 1st, 3rd, and 9th Armies speared their way to the Elbe and arrived at mid-month, with the 1st Army taking the city of Leipzig just before reaching the river. The troops had gone as far as Eisenhower had ordered. Patton's 3rd Army, however, moved on to Czechoslovakia.

In the far south, the U.S. 7th Army and French 1st Army fought their way into the Bavarian Alps, where the 7th captured the city of Munich on April 30. The two forces learned that the reports of the German plan to mass 100,000 men there for a last stand had been groundless. Either the Germans had never planned such an action or, caught between the fast-moving advances from the west and east, they had been unable to put their troops in place for the action.

But April was also a month of horrors. First, the Germans fought back savagely in the face of the Allied advances, and both sides suffered heavy casualties. Second, the

Allies began stumbling upon the concentration camps that Hitler's Nazi regime had built for the people he considered to be enemies of the state.

From his first days in politics in the 1920s, Hitler had told the Germans that they were a superior race, a "master race," and that they deserved to be the dominant people in Europe. In the years after he came to power in the mid-1930s, the concentration camps took shape. Imprisoned in them were Slavs, Poles, Gypsies, and Jews—all branded as enemies because Hitler thought them racially inferior to the Germans. There, ill-fed, living in filthy conditions, and cruelly treated, they were made to do slave labor for the Nazi state until they died of starvation or exhaustion.

Some news of the camps reached the outside world in the 1930s. But the full truth of their horrors did not emerge until Eisenhower's troops and the Soviets came upon them. Then news reports of what the troops were seeing came flooding out of the war zone to stun the world with word of how like savage beasts Hitler's Nazis had been. As the Allied troops approached, they were struck by the sickening stench of death and unwashed bodies. Then they found clusters of buildings surrounded by barbed-wire fences. Staring out at them from behind the fences were living skeletons—ragged, gaunt, and hollow-eyed prisoners left behind to starve when their German guards had fled in the face of the oncoming Allies.

As terrible as all the camps were, the worst were the ones called the "death camps." These had been used for the "Final Solution," the plan that Hitler put into effect in 1942 to rid Europe of the people whom he detested above all others—the Jews. Mostly located in Poland, the death camps contained barnlike structures that varied in size and could hold from 200 to 2,000 people at a time. Into them, Jewish prisoners of all ages were herded and then killed with poison gas. When all the victims had died, their bodies were thrown into mass graves or carted to nearby giant ovens and cremated. In most of the camps, the arriving soldiers found piles of unburied corpses; in one camp, no fewer than 5,000.

No one will ever know exactly how many people died or were killed in the concentration and death camps. It is known, however, that they numbered in the millions. The Jews alone accounted for more than 6 million of that awful total.

THE LAST DAYS ▪ The closing weeks of April and the first seven days of May saw the German war machine collapse on all fronts. On April 16, Marshal Zhukov's Soviet troops opened their final attack on Berlin. By month's end, they were deep inside the city and reducing it to rubble as they fought their way from street to street.

At the center of the dying Berlin, Hitler spent his final days in a concrete-walled complex of underground offices known as the Bunker. Throughout April, he refused to surrender and avoid further deaths. Insanely, he insisted that his armies fight on to the last man. Finally, however, he realized that Germany lay in ruins and that the days of his reign were over. On April 30, he put a small pistol to his right temple and pulled the trigger.

Just before his death, Hitler handed the dying nation over to Admiral Karl Doenitz, the commander of the German Navy. On May 3, Doenitz sent Admiral Hans-Georg von Friedeberg to sue for peace with General Montgomery at the Britisher's headquarters outside Hamburg. Von Friedeberg bowed to Montgomery's demand for an unconditional surrender of all German troops in northern Germany, Holland, and Denmark. The fighting there ended on May 5.

Top: An American soldier guards a group of Nazi prisoners captured in the surrounding forest. Below: Prisoners at the infamous Dachau concentration camp welcomed U.S. troops by raising a homemade American flag.

Three days earlier, the fighting had ended on yet another front. The American and British armies in Italy, after pushing the German defenders to the nation's far northern region in 1944, opened their final attacks on April 9. Troops of the U.S. 5th Army took the city of Bologna and pushed on toward the Italian border with France, Switzerland, and Austria. The British 8th Army first swept north and then east to Yugoslavia. On May 2, the German high command, knowing that all was lost, surrendered to British General Sir Harold Alexander, the chief of the Allied forces in Italy.

On that same day, Marshal Zhukov brought all of Berlin under his control. Then, on May 5, Admiral von Friedeberg arrived at General Eisenhower's headquarters in Rheims, France, to negotiate an overall surrender. He was joined the next day by General Alfred Jodl, Germany's chief of military operations. The two men agreed to an unconditional surrender. The surrender document was prepared and handed to the grim-faced Jodl. He signed it at 2:41 A.M. on May 7, 1945.

It was a date that would go down in the history of the war as V-E Day, meaning "Victory in Europe."

General Jodl signs the unconditional surrender.

ADMIRAL KARL DOENITZ

Admiral Doenitz commanded the German Navy. Just before Adolf Hitler committed suicide, he handed over the reins of the German government to the admiral. Doenitz sent Admiral Hans-Georg von Friedeberg and General Alfred Jodl to arrange a surrender with the allies.

THREE:
THE PHILIPPINE
ISLANDS

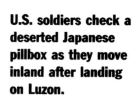

Two major American campaigns marked the final months of the war in the Pacific. General Douglas MacArthur invaded Luzon, the largest island in the Philippines, and then brought all of the nation's islands under his control. At the same time, Admiral Chester W. Nimitz moved north toward Japan and captured the islands of Iwo Jima and Okinawa.

THE INVASION OF LUZON ▪ MacArthur's attack on the Philippines began in late 1944, when his troops invaded the island of Leyte and then moved on to Mindoro. Mindoro lay just off the southwestern tip of Luzon, the largest of the Philippine group and the general's next target. He had air strips built on Mindoro so that he could send bombers to cripple the enemy installations on Luzon before invading the island.

January 1945 was just a few days old when an armada of some 1,000 ships—troop carriers and escort warships—sailed up the west coast of Luzon to Lingayen Gulf. Crowded aboard the transports were the men of Lt. General Walter Kreuger's U.S. 6th Army. They landed on January 9. Exactly three years and twenty days earlier, on December 21, 1941, a massive Japanese force had stormed into the Gulf and had set about crushing the American and Filipino troops defending the island. Now the roles were reversed.

U.S. soldiers check a deserted Japanese pillbox as they move inland after landing on Luzon.

To their surprise, the invading troops met with little enemy fire. The enemy units along the beaches quickly retreated before the onslaught. By day's end, some 70,000 Americans were ashore, with thousands more to follow.

Though more than 275,000 Japanese troops were manning Luzon, there was a reason why they met the invasion with little fire. Their commander, General Tomoyuki Yamashita, planned to fight a purely defensive war, hoping to hold the invaders at bay for as long as possible. Consequently, he did not station a strong force on the Gulf itself. Rather, he placed many of his troops around what he knew would be the chief American target—the capital city of Manila—and on nearby Bataan Peninsula. The two were located opposite each other on giant Manila Bay.

Once ashore, Kreuger immediately began marching south toward Manila some 110 miles away. His men did not run into any hard fighting until, nearing the city, they reached Clark Field, which had been an American air base before the war. Here Kreuger assigned one division to the job of taking the field, while ordering the rest of the troops to continue south. By late January they were approaching Manila.

The closing days of the month saw two new invasion forces strike Luzon. The first arrived on January 29. Its men rushed ashore on the island's west coast just north of Bataan Peninsula. Their assignment was to take the peninsula and keep the enemy troops there from knifing over to reinforce the defenders at Manila. In 1942, the U.S. and Filipino troops on Bataan, outnumbered and with their ammunition running out, had held off the advancing Japanese for four months. The peninsula was now retaken in just ten days.

On January 31, as the fighting on Bataan was starting, the second invasion force landed south of Manila. The capi-

Luzon

*Lingayen
Gulf*

Clark Airfield ○

Manila ●

Bataan

*Manila
Bay*

Corregidor

Cavite ●

Lamon Bay

*Philippine
Sea*

*South
China Sea*

Mindoro

P H I L I P P I N E S

Samar

Panay

Negros

Palawan

*Sulu
Sea*

Mindanao

tal was now caught between U.S. troops pressing in from both the north and south.

THE BATTLE FOR MANILA AND CORREGIDOR ▪ General Kreuger's men reached the outskirts of Manila on February 3. There now followed a month of vicious fighting in which the Japanese gave up the city street by street. An example of how stubbornly they fought was seen on the day an American unit surrounded the walled area that marked the ancient city of Manila. Barricaded inside were 2,000 Japanese soldiers. Trapped with them were about 5,000 Filipino citizens. The U.S. commander, using a loudspeaker, urged the enemy troops to lay down their arms and avoid needless bloodshed. But the Japanese refused. A week later, the area was reduced to smoking rubble and was in American hands. Almost all the Japanese and the Filipino citizens were dead.

On February 16, U.S. paratroopers dropped onto the small island of Corregidor out in Manila Bay and were joined by units landing from the bay itself. It was here, on this 1,735-acre expanse of rock with its network of gun emplacements and underground tunnels, that the Americans had made their last stand against the enemy invaders in early 1942. Now the Japanese on the island were the ones making a last stand.

It was a last stand that dragged on for ten days. In that time, the Americans battled their way toward the enemy headquarters in the tunnel system at the center of the island, with the Japanese defenders stubbornly fighting them every inch of the way. At last, admitting that defeat was inevitable, they blew up their main ammunition dump. The thunderous blast killed more than 250 men. Fifty-two were Americans. Some 200 were Japanese soldiers stationed in the tunnels.

General Douglas MacArthur tours the tunnels of Corregidor after the American victory there.

By March 3, 1945, the organized resistance in Manila came to an end, though some Japanese soldiers, individually or in small groups, continued to fight on for a time. The same held true on Corregidor, where one of the strangest incidents in the postwar months occurred. On January 1, 1946, some four months after Japan's surrender, twenty Japanese soldiers emerged from one of Corregidor's deepest tunnels and gave themselves up. They had been in hiding and had not learned that the war was over until the night before, when one of their number had sneaked outside in search of water and had come upon a discarded newspaper containing reports of a world now at peace.

The taking of Manila did not mark the end of the fighting on Luzon. In the next months, MacArthur's men fought to unseat the Japanese units entrenched in Luzon's rural areas. At the same time, U.S. forces landed on the surrounding islands of Panay, Negros, Cebu, and Mindanao. Many of the nation's smallest islands also fell, some to the Americans with the help of Filipino guerrilla fighters, and some to the guerrillas by themselves.

In July, General MacArthur was able to announce that the fighting in the Philippines was at last at an end. The battle for the island chain had cost his forces some 60,600 casualties. The Japanese toll had been far worse—400,000 men killed or taken captive. Of that total, 300,000 had lost their lives.

As the general was making his announcement, heavy fighting was also coming to a close far to his north. There, beginning back in February, the forces under the command of Admiral Chester W. Nimitz had invaded two islands close to the Japanese homeland—Iwo Jima and Okinawa.

FOUR:
IWO JIMA AND
OKINAWA

Iwo Jima is a small, barren island of volcanic rock lying about 750 miles south of Tokyo, Japan's capital city. Why was this 8-square-mile chunk of rock so important to Admiral Nimitz on his thrust toward Japan?

The answer began with the fact that, since late 1944, B-29 bombers had been attacking the Japanese homeland from bases on distant Pacific islands that the Americans had earlier captured, among them Guam and Tinian. The distance back to the bases was dangerously great for bombers that had been damaged in the raids. Nimitz saw that Iwo Jima could provide them with fields for emergency landings. In addition, it could be used as a base for bombers of its own.

The commanding general on Iwo Jima, Tadamichi Kuribayashi, also recognized the value of the island to the Americans. Certain that they would attempt an invasion there, he set about fortifying the barren clump of rock. He built his first line of defense behind a long stretch of beach on the southeastern coast. Most of the island's coastline was marked by high bluffs that fell steeply to the sea. The beach was the only spot where invading troops could land.

Making up that first line of defense were artillery batteries, machine-gun nests, and concrete pillboxes. Kuribayashi also established defensive positions elsewhere, especially in the hundreds of caves that dotted the island. His 21,000 troops were in place when the American invasion fleet finally swept into view. They were under orders to defend their posts to the last man.

THE BATTLE FOR IWO JIMA ▪ Dawn was breaking on February 19 when the invasion fleet approached Iwo Jima in the company of twenty-three warships. Landing craft dropped down the sides of the troop transports, and the first of the invaders—men from the 4th and 5th Marine Divisions—began to pour ashore. They would be joined in a few days by fellow Marines from the 3rd Division. In time, 60,000 Marines would be fighting on Iwo Jima.

The first arrivals encountered no enemy fire as they trudged across a beach of black volcanic ash. On its far side, they came to a 15-foot-high earthen shelf that separated them from the land beyond. They began to climb over the shelf.

U.S. Marines move up from the beach on Iwo Jima. In the background is Mount Suribachi, which would become the scene of bitter fighting.

GENERAL HOLLAND SMITH

General Smith commanded the Marine force that invaded Iwo Jima. To his troops, he was known as "Howlin' Mad" Smith.

Suddenly, when the men were exposed on the top of the shelf, the Japanese opened fire. The air was filled with the terrible thunder and rattle of cannon, machine guns, and rifles. Instantly, the Marines began to fall. But, despite the deadly fire, more and more landing craft pitched up to the shore throughout the day. More and more Marines crawled over the ledge. By nightfall, though nearly 600 of their number lay dead, the invaders had fought their way off the beach.

In the next days, they spread inland. Some headed west across the island. Some moved north. And some turned south and began climbing the extinct volcano, Mount Suribachi. Rising to an elevation of 546 feet, Suribachi was the highest spot on Iwo Jima. It stood alongside the invasion beach.

For three days, the Marines struggled up Suribachi's slopes, fighting their way past artillery emplacements and machine-gun nests. When the troops reached the summit, a dozen men raised a small American flag. An hour later, a larger flag was hoisted in its place by six men. Present at the second raising was Joe Rosenthal, an Associated Press photographer. He snapped a picture of the men as they thrust the flagpole into the rocky summit and sent the flag upward to unfurl against the smoke-stained sky. Rosenthal's photograph became one of the most famous taken during the war.

During the next weeks, the Marines who moved west and north into the island fought their way over barren hills and through rock-strewn valleys. All the while, they faced troops who stubbornly chose to die rather than surrender. Daily, the Marines had to clear Japanese foxholes and machine-gun nests with grenades and bayonets. Daily, they had to use flamethrowers to drive the enemy out of the myriad caves that blocked their path. They began christening the spots

This famous photograph of troops raising the American flag on Suribachi inspired the United States Marine Corps War Memorial in Washington, D.C.

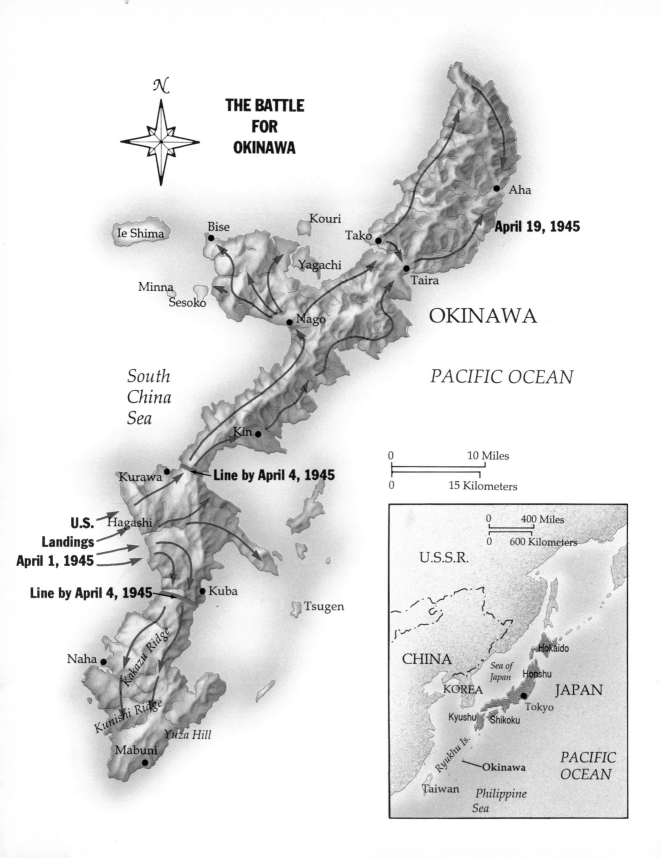

N

THE BATTLE FOR OKINAWA

April 19, 1945

Aha

Kouri

Bise

Tako

Ie Shima

Yagachi

Taira

Minna

Sesoko

Nago

OKINAWA

South China Sea

PACIFIC OCEAN

Kin

0   10 Miles

Kurawa

Line by April 4, 1945

0   15 Kilometers

U.S. Landings April 1, 1945

Hagashi

Line by April 4, 1945

Kuba

Tsugen

0   400 Miles

0   600 Kilometers

Naha

Kakazu Ridge

U.S.S.R.

Hokaido

Kunishi Ridge

CHINA

Sea of Japan

Honshu

JAPAN

Yuza Hill

KOREA

Tokyo

Mabuni

Kyushu

Shikoku

Ryukyu Is.

Okinawa

Taiwan

Philippine Sea

PACIFIC OCEAN

of the heaviest fighting with grim nicknames—the Meat Grinder, the Mincer, and Bloody Gulch.

But no matter how fierce the enemy resistance, it could not hold the Marines at bay. The Marines who were moving to the northern area reached their destination and brought it under control by the end of February. The men thrusting west pressed on until they reached the far side of the island and closed in on the cave that served as Kuribayashi's headquarters. Shamed by his defeat, the general committed suicide. With his death, the defense of Iwo Jima came to an end. Of Kuribayashi's 21,000 men, just over 1,000 remained alive. Only about 200 surrendered to the Marines, however. The rest concealed themselves in their caves, with all but two remaining there for weeks or months before giving up. Those last two did not emerge until six years after the war had ended.

For the Marines, the Battle of Iwo Jima recorded the greatest death toll in the history of their Corps: 6,821 lives. The Navy suffered the loss of 900 sailors.

THE BATTLE FOR OKINAWA ▪ Okinawa was the last stop on the American thrust to Japan. A long and narrow island of 454 square miles, it lay a mere 350 miles from Kyushu, the southernmost of Japan's main home islands.

When captured, Okinawa would serve as the base for the invasion of Japan itself. It would provide airfields for bombing attacks prior to the invasion. It would house all the supplies needed for the operation. And it would serve as the jumping-off spot for the Japan-bound troops.

The invasion of Okinawa began on April 1, 1945. Making the landing that Easter Sunday morning along a stretch of beach on the island's southwestern coast were 60,000 men

of the U.S. 10th Army, a combined Army and Marine force. Within a few weeks, 186,000 Americans would be fighting on Okinawa.

The landing itself gave the troops little trouble because the island's defense lines were located to the north and south of the invasion site. The Americans immediately split into two groups. The Marines marched north; the Army units turned south.

In the next days, the Marines proved to be the luckier of the two forces. Though fighting hard, they found that they were not up against Okinawa's main line of defense. That main line stretched across the island south of the invasion beach. By April 18, the Marines had reached Okinawa's northernmost shores and had subdued the defenders there.

To the south, the Army troops ran into a growing resistance as they approached the island's main defense line. They were soon inching through a maze of pillboxes, machine-gun nests, and fortified caves. The fighting resembled that on Iwo Jima and was just as vicious. The Americans leveled the pillboxes with artillery and mortar fire, hurled grenades into the machine-gun nests, cleared the foxholes with bayonets, and aimed flamethrowers into the heavily defended caves. Whenever they could not empty a cave of the enemy, they sealed its mouth with explosives. It was estimated that 20,000 Japanese died in the sealed caves.

The battle in the south raged through April and May. In early June, the Army troops, now joined by Marine units, reached the hilly foot of Okinawa. Here, again with their flamethrowers and bayonets, they spent ten bloody days taking two final strongholds—one on Kunishi Ridge, and the other on Yuza Hill. Once beyond the two, they closed in on

Ships crowd the waters around Okinawa as the Americans bring troops and supplies ashore.

the enemy headquarters at the village of Mabuni, reaching it by June 21. Two days later, with the surrender of several thousand Japanese soldiers, the organized resistance on the island collapsed. The fighting was officially declared at an end on July 3.

During all the weeks that the Americans were moving south, the navy ships that had escorted the invasion force to Okinawa stood offshore. They bombarded enemy positions on the island and flooded the beach with supplies. As they worked, they were hit by an unending series of deadly air attacks.

Carrying out the attacks were kamikaze planes. The term *kamikaze* means ''Divine Wind.'' It refers to typhoon winds that, in the thirteenth century, had destroyed the ships of the Mongol ruler Kublai Khan as they were sailing to invade Japan. The kamikaze planes were actually flying bombs that were flown by fanatical young pilots who were willing to commit suicide for their country. On taking off, the pilots knew they would never return home. Their mission was to dive into the U.S. ships and die in the explosions that ripped their targets to pieces.

The kamikazes were used in desperation when Japan's war leaders realized that their forces were being overwhelmed by American strength. The suicide planes were first tried during the invasion of the Philippines. Only a few had been unleashed, but they had done extensive harm. They had sunk two U.S. carriers and a destroyer and had damaged a number of other warships.

Now, at Okinawa, they struck in force. Flying in from Japan, over 1,900 of the suicide planes smashed into the American fleet. They sank or disabled more than thirty war-

A Japanese kamikaze plane attacks the USS *Missouri* off Okinawa in April 1945.

ships; among the vessels heavily damaged were the battleship *Mississippi* and the heavy cruiser *Louisville*. At one point, the battleship *Yamato* left Japan and sailed to Okinawa for the purpose of joining 5,000 kamikazes in a coordinated attack. But U.S. Navy planes intercepted the warship and pounded it with torpedoes and bombs. It rolled over and went to the bottom.

When the battle for Okinawa finally came to an end, 107,500 Japanese were dead. The American losses totaled 7,613 soldiers dead, and 4,900 sailors lost in the kamikaze and other air assaults. Altogether, including Okinawa's civilian population, the fighting had claimed a quarter of a million lives.

Neither the Americans nor the Japanese knew it at the time, but the terrible fighting on Okinawa had not been necessary. Its purpose had been to pave the way for two invasions of Japan itself. Those invasions were destined never to take place.

FIVE:
A SPLIT-SECOND
AT HIROSHIMA

The B-29 Superfort swept along the runway on the island of Tinian. Rising into the darkness at 2:45 A.M., it swung north toward Japan. In another five hours and twenty-six minutes—at 8:11 A.M., August 6, 1945—it would reach its target, the city of Hiroshima. Riding in the belly of the plane was the cigar-shaped atomic bomb known as "Little Boy."

THE MANHATTAN PROJECT ▪ "Little Boy" was the product of secret work that began in 1939 when physicist Albert Einstein told President Franklin Roosevelt of the advances being made by German scientists in splitting the atom. At the time, atomic research was being conducted in a number of countries, including the United States. Einstein explained that the Germans were far ahead of everyone in the research and had succeeded in splitting the uranium atom in their laboratories.

The splitting could unleash a fantastic amount of energy. Einstein warned the president that Germany's achievement could lead to the creation of an atomic bomb. One such bomb would have the power to devastate a wide area and kill thousands of people.

America was still at peace in 1939. But Roosevelt knew that Germany must not become the only nation with such a

terrible weapon. He decided that the United States must do everything possible to develop an atomic bomb. The development must take place in complete secrecy; Germany must not get wind of what was happening.

The decision led to two immediate tasks. First, quantities of needed uranium were located and brought home. Next, an army of scientists began to develop an efficient method for extracting from the uranium the radioactive substances that were required for the bomb.

In 1942, a program called the Manhattan Project was created to handle the next two jobs in the bomb's development. The first was the awesome task of building two giant atomic plants to extract the radioactive substances in sufficient amounts to fire the bomb—and extract them quickly enough for use in the near future.

The direction of the Manhattan Project was assigned to General Leslie R. Groves. A hard-driving army engineer, he had the two monster plants built in a matter of months—one at Oak Ridge, Tennessee, and the other at Hanford, Washington. By 1944, the two plants were beginning to turn out ample amounts of the needed substances.

The Project now turned to its final task. Groves brought an army of top scientists to a secret installation at Los Alamos, New Mexico. Their number included not only Americans but also Britishers, Canadians, and representatives from several European countries that Hitler had overrun. Supervised by U.S. physicist Robert Oppenheimer, they set about designing the bomb itself. They worked so quickly that they were ready to test an experimental model in mid-1945. They hoisted it to the top of a 100-foot tower in a desolate section of the New Mexico desert.

Physicist J. Robert Oppenheimer and General Leslie R. Groves, director of the Manhattan Project, inspect the aftermath of the test explosion. The iron bars are all that remain of a 100-foot tower.

The bomb was triggered at 5:29:04 on the morning of July 16. Instantly, a force equal to 18,000 tons of TNT was unleashed. The tower evaporated. A ball of blinding white light shattered the darkness. A hot wind swept across the desert. As the white light faded, a monstrous curtain of smoke and dust rose into the air and turned itself into a mushroom-shaped cloud. Left behind in the burned sandy earth was a crater half a mile wide and ten feet deep.

The nuclear age was born in those terrifying moments. And the final fate of Japan in World War II was sealed.

THE TERRIBLE QUESTION ▪ At the time of the test explosion, America was preparing to invade the Japanese homeland. That preparation saw fleets of U.S. bombers strike the nation. They came from carriers at sea, from Iwo Jima and Okinawa, and from such islands as Saipan and Tinian deep in the Pacific. Daily, they pounded Japan's military installations and industrial cities to dust. Only a few enemy aircraft came up to intercept them. Japan's supply of aviation fuel was running low and was being saved to help fight off the invasion that the Japanese realized must soon come.

Actually, two invasions were planned. The first would strike Kyushu, the southernmost of the main home islands, on November 1, 1945. The second would follow in March 1946, and would send troops into Honshu, Japan's largest island and the home of the nation's capital. Massive forces would carry out the invasions. Estimates held that the two operations would result in death and injury for over a million American fighting men.

The loss of life would be great despite the fact that Japan was being deeply wounded by the air bombings. U.S. military planners knew there were 1 million troops in the home islands. And they knew the Japanese soldiers to be stubborn foes who preferred death to surrender. The homeland troops—and the civilian population—could be expected to defend their country with all their might.

And so, once the atomic bomb had been successfully tested, America's military and political leaders had to face a terrible question. Should this new weapon, which would take the lives of thousands within seconds, be dropped on a Japanese city in the hope of bringing the war to a sudden end?

The question caused much disagreement among the nation's leaders. Some felt that the bomb should not be used for fear the world would condemn the United States for unleashing such an awful weapon. Others held that it should be used but that the Japanese people should be warned of its coming. Still others urged that it be exploded in a demonstration for the enemy leaders. Surely, even as stubborn as they were, they would sue for peace once they saw its awesome power.

The final decision lay with America's new president, Harry S. Truman. Truman, who had been serving as vice president, moved into the White House in April, when President Roosevelt died suddenly of a cerebral hemorrhage and plunged the country into deep mourning for its wartime leader. With the help of a committee selected to advise him in atomic matters, Truman decided that the bomb had to be dropped. He saw it as the only means of convincing Japan that all was lost. The bomb would take thousands of innocent lives, but it would save a far greater number—all the American and Japanese lives that would be lost in the homeland invasions. Truman reached his decision in June.

In July, he met with Russia's Joseph Stalin and Britain's Winston Churchill at the city of Potsdam, Germany, to discuss a series of postwar matters. (In the last days of the meeting, Churchill was replaced by a new prime minister, Clement Atlee.) During the conference, Mr. Truman told his fellow leaders of the atomic bomb. As a result, they joined him in issuing a statement that called on Japan to surrender unconditionally or face "prompt and utter destruction."

Actually, some weeks earlier, the Japanese had sent a peace offer to the United States via Russia (which had not yet entered the Pacific war). But they had wanted their surrender to contain a special condition—the agreement to allow their emperor, Hirohito, to remain on the throne after the war. Hirohito did not rule the country, but he was revered as a godlike figure by his people. The United States had rejected the offer and had demanded an unconditional surrender. Now, the announcement at Potsdam repeated that demand. The Japanese met the announcement with silence.

HIROSHIMA: 8:16:02 A.M., AUGUST 6, 1945 ▪ Long before Mr. Truman's decision, plans were being made to drop the atomic bomb in case it had to be used. A special bombing unit, the 509th Composite Group, was formed and began to train for the mission. Flying out of Wendover Air Base in Utah, the Group pilots daily took their B-29 Superforts aloft to 30,000 feet and practiced dropping heavy steel casings— empty bombs that they nicknamed "pumpkins"—on various targets.

The pilots realized that theirs was a special mission. But they were not told that the mission was to drop an atomic bomb and that only one plane would be used for the task;

British Prime Minister Clement Atlee, U.S. President Harry S. Truman, and Soviet leader Joseph Stalin at Potsdam

the rest were to serve as back-up ships in case they were needed. They were told only that, as soon as they dropped their ''pumpkins,'' they were to flee the target area as fast as possible. They had to be a safe eight miles away in forty-three seconds.

In April, the 509th was moved to the giant air base on the island of Tinian, which was located some 1,000 miles southeast of Japan. At the same time, military planners in Washington, D.C., were selecting possible targets for the Group's mission. Four cities were chosen on the basis that they had escaped the U.S. air attacks thus far and so would reveal to the Japanese leaders the full extent of the bomb's damage. The cities were Hiroshima, Kokura, Niigata, and Nagasaki.

A secret message went out to Tinian in mid-summer. The 509th was to strike one of the target cities with a ''special bomb'' as soon as the weather permitted in early August.

The city finally named for the attack was Hiroshima, on the southeast coast of Honshu. The Superfort that was to make the attack was to be piloted by Colonel Paul W. Tibbets, Jr. It bore his mother's name, Enola Gay.

The *Enola Gay,* with the cigar-shaped ''Little Boy'' in its bomb bay, cleared Tinian at 2:45 A.M., August 6. As Tibbets took the B-29 to 9,000 feet, Navy Captain William ''Deac'' Ramsey began to arm the four-ton bomb. It had not been armed earlier to avoid a deadly explosion if Tibbets crashed on takeoff.

The colonel, accompanied by two B-29s whose crews would observe the bombing, held the *Enola Gay* at 9,000 feet to conserve fuel on the five-hour flight to Hiroshima. On sighting the Japanese coast, he began climbing and was at

Col. Paul Tibbets, Jr., waves from the cockpit of the *Enola Gay* before takeoff on August 6, 1945.

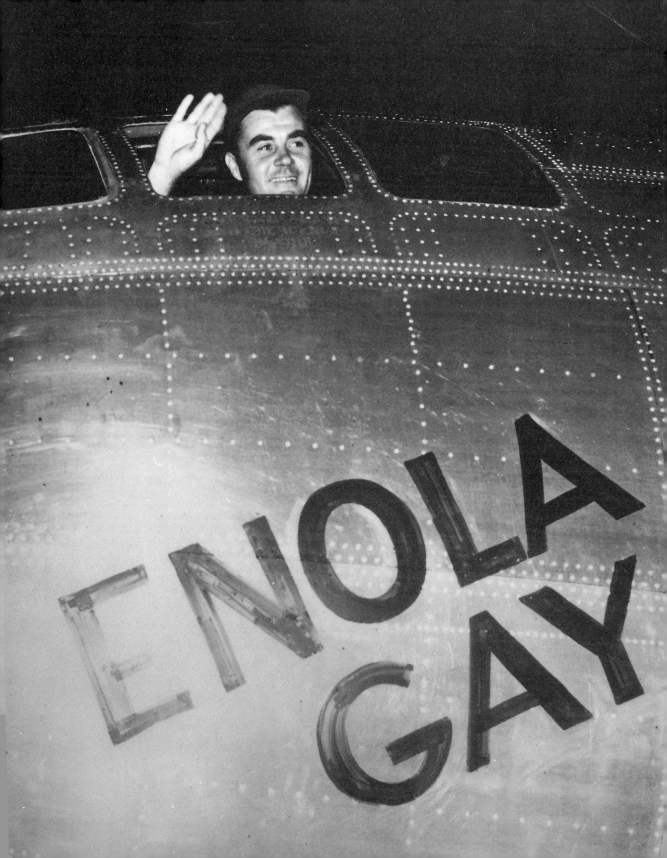

31,600 feet when he swept in on Hiroshima. He started his bombing run at 8:11 A.M. The Superfort's bomb bay doors opened at 8:15:17. "Little Boy" plunged down through the warm morning air.

Banking hard, Tibbets raced away from the target area. He counted off the forty-three seconds to detonation. Nothing happened at the forty-third second, but, an instant later, at 8:16:02, "Little Boy" exploded 1,850 feet above Hiroshima.

The sky turned a blinding white. Smoke and dust boiled 40,000 feet into the air and changed into the mushroom-shaped cloud that would soon become known the world over. On the ground, buildings were ripped apart by a sun-hot heat. Thousands of people vanished in the heat, leaving behind only dark shadows on the ground where they had been standing. Those who were not killed instantly were left with their skin in burned shreds.

Aboard the *Enola Gay*, co-pilot Captain Robert Lewis stared back at the boiling cloud. When he spoke, his words would match those of countless people in the future when they thought of the dangers promised by the nuclear age:

"My God, what have we done?"

The atomic bomb dropped on the Japanese city of Hiroshima opened a new and terrifying era in history. The atomic blast created a mushroom cloud that rose 40,000 feet over Hiroshima. On the ground, destruction stretched for miles.

SIX:
THE FINAL
MOMENTS

Some 180,000 people died, were injured, or vanished in the terrible white flash at Hiroshima. Of their number, 70,000 were dead or presumed dead.

President Truman had expected the Japanese war ministers to surrender immediately. But, to his surprise, several days passed without a word from them. There was a reason for their silence. They were caught in a heated debate over what to do in the face of a new and devastating weapon. Some urged a surrender. Others wanted to fight on, saying that the United States surely did not have enough of the new bombs to destroy all of Japan; there were still ample troops at home to fight off an invasion. And most balked at the idea of an unconditional surrender because it promised to remove the revered Emperor Hirohito from his throne.

President Truman stirred impatiently at the Japanese silence. He was more than convinced that the atomic bomb was the only way to end the war with the least loss of American life. And so, to prod the enemy to a decision, he ordered that a second bomb be dropped.

The scientists at Los Alamos had designed two atomic bombs—"Little Boy" and a football-shaped model called "Fat Man." On the president's orders, "Fat Man" was placed aboard a B-29 at Tinian on August 9. Bearing the name *Bock's*

The USS *Missouri* was the scene of the formal Japanese surrender on September 2, 1945.

Car and piloted by Major Charles Sweeney, the Superfort flew to the city of Nagasaki on Japan's southernmost island, Kyushu. There, "Fat Man" hurtled down out of the sky and burst 1,650 feet above the city. Killed in its flash were 35,000 people, and thousands more were left cruelly burned.

Still the ministers did not announce a surrender. They continued to argue through days of heavy conventional bombings by U.S. planes. At last, late at night on August 12, they were summoned for a conference with Emperor Hirohito. He told them that he wished the war to end immediately. Though he did not actually rule the country and so could not order a surrender, his words always bore great weight. The ministers nodded in silence.

Then, little more than a day later, the emperor broadcast a radio message to his people. It was a message that was quickly relayed to the rest of the world: Japan could not continue sacrificing the lives of its people in a lost war. The nation would no longer fight on.

The date in the United States was August 14, 1945—V-J Day, for "Victory in Japan."

EMPEROR HIROHITO

Hirohito's radio broadcast of Japan's surrender marked the first time his people had heard his voice. Although the surrender was unconditional, the emperor was allowed to remain on the throne. However, his status changed: He was no longer a godlike being, but a symbol of the Japanese state.

AT PEACE AGAIN • The word of the Japanese surrender, as had the end of the European fighting back in May, triggered celebrations throughout the United States. Americans everywhere knew that the greatest war in the history of their country—and the world—was at last over. No more lives had to be lost. Too many had already been sacrificed.

America had contributed 16,353,659 men and women to the fighting. Of that number, 407,316 had lost their lives—a total that was made up of deaths in battle and deaths from other causes. The toll for the Army and its Air Force (the latter had yet to be designated a separate branch of the service) stood at 318,274. For the Navy, it came to 62,614; the Marine Corps, 24,511; and the Coast Guard, 1,917.

But, though its losses were heartbreaking, the United States was among the more fortunate of the Allied nations. Others had suffered far greater military losses. Russia sustained the greatest number of all—7.5 million dead. China came next, with some 2.2 million dead. Great Britain's death toll stood at approximately 357,000. The loss of life recorded by the British Commonwealth nations of Australia, Canada, and New Zealand totaled just over 80,600. The British holding India reported some 32,000 deaths.

On the enemy side in Europe, some 3.5 million German troops were dead. Italy's losses came to about 200,000. Listed as dead in the Pacific were 1.5 million Japanese fighters.*

Altogether, fifty-seven nations, both large and small, had fought in the war. In total, they had lost more than 15 million soldiers, sailors, and airmen.

*Should you read further about World War II, you will find that the statistics for military deaths differ among various sources. The figures listed above were collected chiefly from the *New American Encyclopedia* (Grolier Incorporated, 1991) and *The World Almanac and Book of Facts: 1993* (Pharos Books, 1992).

The military losses, however, tell only part of the terrible story of World War II. The conflict had not only been the greatest in history, but had also been the most vicious—this because it had marked the first time that cities had endured wholesale bombings from the air. And it had witnessed the murder of some 6 million of Europe's Jewish population at the hands of Germany's Nazi regime. In all, though the exact total would never be known, more than 50 million people—both military personnel and civilians—were killed during the years of fighting. Millions more were uprooted from their homes or were left living amid the rubble of bombed cities. Years would pass before their lives returned to normal and their nations rebuilt themselves.

THIRTY MINUTES ABOARD THE *MISSOURI* • The battleship *Missouri,* surrounded by a gleaming armada of U.S. warships, rode at anchor in Tokyo Bay on Sunday morning, September 2, 1945. Hundreds of newsmen and sailors crowded its decks and gun turrets. All eyes were on the high-ranking officers who stood on the quarterdeck.

The officers wore the uniforms of the nations that had been involved in the Pacific war—the United States, Great Britain, China, Australia, Canada, New Zealand, the Netherlands, France, and the Soviet Union. The Soviet officers were on board because Stalin, in keeping with the agreements made at Yalta, had declared war against Japan on August 8.

The officers stood in a U formation around a long table in the middle of the deck. The table was covered with green cloth and had a chair to each side. Lying on it were two copies of the surrender document that, once signed, would bring World War II to an official close. One copy was for the Allies and was bound in leather. The other, bound in canvas, was meant for the Japanese.

At 8:55, the destroyer *Lansdowne* came alongside the *Missouri*. Aboard was a delegation of eleven Japanese military officers and statesmen. The group was led by Foreign Minister Mamoru Shigemitsu. He slowly led his delegation across the quarterdeck and came to a stop before the table. Immediately, General Douglas MacArthur, who was to command the Pacific area in peacetime, appeared. He stepped to the side of the table opposite Shigemitsu and stood there quietly while a chaplain spoke an invocation and the "Star Spangled Banner" was broadcast over the *Missouri*'s loudspeakers.

Then the general, wearing a simple uniform without service ribbons, began to speak. He said that the warring powers were here this morning to restore peace to the world. It was his hope that they were not meeting in a spirit of distrust, malice, or hatred. Rather, he hoped they were gathering in a spirit that would bring a better world—a world of freedom, tolerance, and justice.

His words astonished some members of the Japanese delegation. They thought that MacArthur would behave like a strutting conquerer and spend his time humiliating them and their country. Instead, he spoke of everyone striving together for a better world.

When he had finished, the general signaled Shigemitsu to sign the surrender documents. Yoshijiro Umeza, the chief of the Japanese imperial staff, followed suit. MacArthur then had the representatives of the Allied nations step forward and put their signatures in place.

Top: Foreign Minister Mamoru Shigemitsu, Gen. Yoshijiro Umeza, and the rest of the Japanese delegation aboard the *Missouri*. Shigemitsu had lost a leg some years earlier and walked with the aid of a cane and an artificial limb. Below: The Japanese sign the surrender.

At last, MacArthur himself sat down at the table and signed his name to the documents. He used five pens to do so. Of the five, one was to go to West Point, one to Annapolis, and a third to his family. One pen each went to two men who stood in places of honor behind MacArthur—U.S. General Jonathan Wainwright and British General Arthur Percival. Wainwright had been in command at Corregidor, and Percival at Singapore, when both places were overwhelmed by the Japanese in 1942. The two men had spent the war as prisoners.

When the signing was completed, MacArthur came to his feet and said, "These proceedings are now closed." The Japanese silently left the *Missouri*. It was now 9:25 A.M. The ceremony had lasted just thirty minutes.

World War II was at an end.

Millions of refugees were resettled in the years just after the war. Among them were this Japanese boy (inset) and these Polish families.

EPILOGUE: THE YEARS SINCE 1945

The American people began the postwar years with deep feelings of hope and dread. They were filled with the hope that the defeat of two tyrannical powers and the establishment of the United Nations would make the world safe from bloodshed for the rest of their lives. But there was a sense of dread when the growth of Soviet communism and America's dedication to opposing it seemed to promise the exact opposite—the outbreak of a nuclear holocaust that could claim millions of lives in seconds and put an end to civilization.

Americans also began the postwar years with the knowledge that their nation, though it had lost thousands of its people in the fighting and had seen thousands of others wounded, had been one of the most fortunate of participants in World War II. No city in the continental United States had been bombed into ruins, nor had any state ever been a battleground. The country was undamaged and rich in the goods that all the war-ravaged nations had lost.

In 1948, the United States put its wealth to work to help the nations of Western Europe restore their shattered economies. Instituted that year was the European Recovery Program, which was popularly called the Marshall Plan in honor of Secretary of State George C. Marshall, who had announced the program during a 1947 speech at Harvard University.

In the years from 1948 to 1953, the plan saw sixteen European nations receive $13.15 billion in American aid not only for the rebuilding of their economies but also for the rebirth of trade with each other and worldwide. In addition to the Marshall Plan, the United States made loans in the billions of dollars to other countries to help their recovery. Among the recipients were China, Greece, and Turkey.

Across the world, General MacArthur was assigned the task of heading the occupation of a battered Japan. Under his direction, the nation disarmed its military forces and adopted reform measures that distributed its land more fairly among the people. MacArthur was also instrumental in guiding Japan to a new and democratic constitution.

But trouble soon loomed in a world so recently returned to peace. By 1947, the Cold War was taking shape. On one side were the United States and the countries of Western Europe. On the other were the Communist nations headed by the Soviet Union. The Cold War came by its name because, while never plunging the two sides into an open war with each other, it plagued them with a string of dangerous crises and conflicts that stained the rest of the century.

The Cold War finally ended in the late 1980s, with the collapse of communism in the Soviet Union and a warming relationship with the United States. By then, the people of both nations—and of the entire world—had come to understand that their century, marked throughout by wars, rebellions, and political upheavals, was to be remembered as one of the most turbulent in all history.

BIBLIOGRAPHY

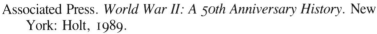

Associated Press. *World War II: A 50th Anniversary History*. New York: Holt, 1989.

Bailey, Thomas A. *The American Pageant: A History of the Republic*. Boston: D. C. Heath, 1956.

Dolan, Edward F. *Adolf Hitler: A Portrait in Tyranny*. New York: Dodd, Mead, 1981.

———*Victory in Europe: The Fall of Hitler's Germany*. New York: Franklin Watts, 1988.

Gilbert, Martin. *The Second World War: A Complete History*. New York: Holt, 1989.

Hall, John Whitney, editor. *History of the World: World War I to the Present Day*. London: Bison Books, 1988.

Lawson, Don. *The United States in World War II*. New York: Abelard-Schuman, 1963.

Manchester, William. *American Caesar: Douglas MacArthur, 1880–1964*. Boston: Little, Brown, 1978.

Morison, Samuel Eliot, and Henry Steele Commager. *The Growth of the American Republic, 1865–1950*, 7th edition. New York: Oxford University Press, 1980.

Shirer, William L. *The Rise and Fall of the Third Reich*. New York: Simon & Schuster, 1960.

Snyder, Louis L. *World War II*. New York: Franklin Watts, 1981.

Steinberg, Rafael, and the editors of Time-Life Books. *Return to the Philippines*. Alexandria, Va.: Time-Life Books, 1979.

Sulzberger, C. L. *The American Heritage Picture History of World War II*. New York: American Heritage Publishing, 1966.

———*The Rising Sun: The Decline and Fall of the Japanese Empire, 1936–1945*. New York: Random House, 1970.

Toland, John. *The Last 100 Days*. New York: Random House, 1966.

INDEX

Page numbers in *italics* refer to illustrations.

Alexander, Sir Harold, 27
Allies, defined, 7
Atlee, Clement, 52, *53*
Atomic bomb, 47, *48*, 49-52, 54, *56*, 57, 59-60
Australia, 61

Bataan Peninsula, 30
Bavarian Alps, 20, 22
Belgium, 7, 8
Berlin, 17, 20, 21, 24, 27
Bock's Car, 59-60
Bradley, Omar N., 10, 12, *13*
Bratge, Willi, 14, 15
B-29 bombers, 35
Bulge, Battle of the, 8, 9

Canada, 9, 17, 61
China, Japanese invasion of, 5
Churchill, Winston, 21-22, 52
Clark Field, 30
Cold War, 68
Cologne, *9*
Communism, 67, 68
Concentration camps, 23-24, *25*
Corregidor, 32, *33*, 34, 65
Czechoslovakia, 17, 22

Dachau concentration camp, *25*

Death camps, 23-24, *25*
Denmark, 20, 22
Devers, Jacob, 10
Doenitz, Karl, 24, 27

East Prussia, 17
8th Army (British), 27
Einstein, Albert, 47
Eisenhower, Dwight D., 7-10, *13*, 18, 20-22, 27
Elbe River, 20, 22
Enola Gay, 54, *55*, 57

5th Army (U.S.), 27
5th Marine Division (U.S.), 36
Final Solution, 23
1st Army (Canadian), 9, 17
1st Army (French), 10, 18, 20, 22
1st Army (U.S.), 10, 12, 14, 15, 18, 20, 22
509th Composite Group, 52, 54
4th Marine Division (U.S.), 36
France, 7, 10, 18, 20, 22
Friedeburg, Hans-Georg von, 24, 27

Germany, 5
  Battle of the Bulge, 8
  concentration camps, 23-24
  division of, 21